MOVIEMAKERS' FILM CLUB

Be an ACTOR

Bring the Script to LIFE

PowerKiDS press.

New York

by
Alix Wood

Published in 2018 by Rosen Publishing
29 East 21st Street, New York, NY 10010

CATALOGING-IN-PUBLICATION DATA
Names: Wood, Alix.
Title: Be an actor: bring the script to life / Alix Wood.
Description: New York : PowerKids Press, 2018. | Series: Moviemakers' film club | Includes index.
Identifiers: LCCN ISBN 9781538323762 (pbk.) | ISBN 9781538322789 (library bound) | ISBN 9781538323779 (6 pack)
Subjects: LCSH: Acting--Juvenile literature.
Classification: LCC PN2086.W64 2018 | DDC 792.02'26--dc23

Produced for Rosen Publishing by Alix Wood Books
Designed by Alix Wood
Editor: Eloise Macgregor
Editor for Rosen: Kerri O'Donnell
Series consultant: Cameron Browne

Cover, 1, 4, 6, 7, 8, 9, 11, 12, 13, 14 , 16, 20, 21, 22, 23, 24, 26, 27, 28, 29 © Adobe Stock
Images; 10 © A. Hellmann; 15 © Alix Wood; 18 © wavebreakmedia/Shutterstock

Printed in the United States of America
CPSIA compliance information: Batch #BW18PK: For further information contact
Rosen Publishing, New York, New York at 1-800-542-2595.

CONTENTS

Introducing the Actor! 4

Film Acting 6

Getting in Character 8

The Fourth Wall 10

Working in Front of the Camera 12

Working On Set 14

Being Consistent 16

Learning Lines 18

Using Your Voice.................................20

Act Natural 22

Stunts and Combat...............................24

Becoming an Actor 26

Auditions 28

Glossary 30

For More Information 31

Index 32

INTRODUCING THE ACTOR!

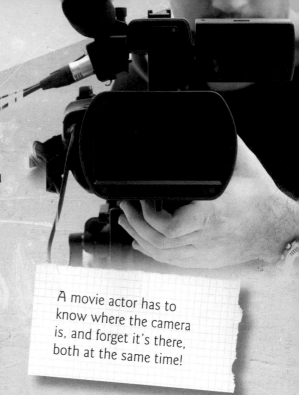

You spent last night reading your lines over and over, making sure you knew them off by heart. You arrived on set early. Now, with hair and makeup ready, you are called onto the **movie set**. All around you there are camera crew members, **lighting technicians**, and **sound recordists**. The director calls "Action!" With a camera inches from your face, you must forget the crew exists, relax, and say your lines. It is not always easy being an actor.

A movie actor has to know where the camera is, and forget it's there, both at the same time!

An actor needs to...

- be able to act
- be creative
- be disciplined
- be able to cope with rejection
- have a good memory for learning parts quickly
- be determined
- have a good understanding of dramatic techniques

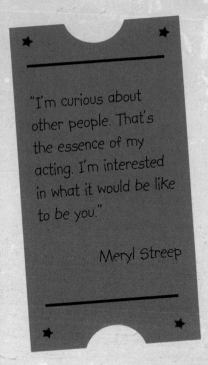

"I'm curious about other people. That's the essence of my acting. I'm interested in what it would be like to be you."

Meryl Streep

Cell Phone Movie School

If you have always wanted to be a film star, try getting together with some friends and making your own movie. You can use a smartphone or any camera that can take video. See if you can find a friend who is interested in directing movies, and one who wants to be a camera operator. You may know people with all kinds of hidden talents, such as doing hair and makeup, making costumes, managing lighting and sound, and even doing special effects. Ask around, pin a flyer on your school bulletin board, and see what happens.

FILM ACTING

Most people have done a little acting, perhaps in a school play or during a drama class. Movie acting is different in many ways from acting on stage. A great theater actor may not be such a great movie actor. They may have to **tone down** their performance for the camera.

The Differences Between Stage and Film Acting

Stage Acting
- Audience reaction lets actors know what lines are working.
- People may compare your acting to past versions of the play.
- Actors must act so people in the theater's back row can see them.
- Your audience may know your lines better than you do!

Film Acting
- There is no audience reacting to your performance.
- Acting should be natural, with no exaggerated sound or movement.
- Actors can play with their lines in the script without the audience noticing. The director will, though!
- The story is often filmed in the wrong order.

Both these actors are acting sad. Can you guess which actor is playing to a distant audience, and which is acting to camera?

Cell Phone Movie School

Sometimes when acting to camera, it is better to not "act" at all. Just thinking what your character is feeling during the scene may be enough. That emotion will come out through your eyes and tiny changes in your expression.

Try it for yourself. Get your camera set up to film a **close-up** of your face, and press record. Think of the happiest time you can remember. Then think of the saddest time you can remember. Don't act, just think. Now run the footage back. Can you see your face change at all?

"Sometimes you're watching a great film actor, and if you stand 10 feet away from them, you're like, '...they're terrible. They're not doing anything.' And then you see the close-up, and ... so much expression is happening. They were acting for that camera and for no one else."

Finn Wittrock

Can you tell which face is thinking sad or happy thoughts?

GETTING IN CHARACTER

Actors need to really get to know the character they are playing. Once they walk around in their character's shoes, they can give a much more believable performance. How to do begin to understand your character? Try asking yourself the questions in the box below. Write down your answers and begin to build your **backstory**.

"Every scene you will ever act begins in the middle, and it is up to you, the actor, to provide what comes before."

Michael Shurtlef

Getting Your Backstory

- **Who am I?** What was your childhood like? Where did you grow up? What good and bad experiences have you had?

- **Where am I?** What is your relationship with the **location** in each scene? Is it your home, or work? Your character would behave in different ways depending on where they were.

- **When is it?** Is the scene set in summer? People can act irritable in the heat. Or perhaps it is set in the past, where people might have different manners than we do now.

Cell Phone Movie School

Start to study actors' **body language**. Body language is the expressions, body posture, gestures, and eye movement that can give away how someone is feeling. Watch a TV show or a movie with the sound off. Can you guess what the actors are saying by their body language? What is it about their acting that gives you that idea? Notice any gestures and expressions, and try to use them in your own acting.

What do you think these girls' body language says about how they are feeling?

You could give your character an accent. Only try this if you are very good at the accent, though. You will have to keep it sounding the same throughout the whole movie.

Don't have many lines? Don't worry, there is still plenty you can do to make your part memorable. Don't make the mistake of thinking that the lines are the only actable part of the script. They are the speakable part of the script. Over 90 percent of human communication is through our actions, not our words. Think about how your character might move, walk, sit, and stand. Watch how people that are like your character behave, and try to copy that in your performance.

THE FOURTH WALL

The first rule of movie acting is "don't look at the camera!" Looking directly at the camera, and therefore, the audience, breaks **the fourth wall**. The term comes from the theater, where the fourth wall is the imaginary wall between the stage and the audience. The audience can see the actors, but the actors must pretend they can't see the audience through the wall.

It must be difficult to pretend a huge audience like this one isn't there!

Not looking at the camera can be quite difficult. In everyday life, when someone photographs or films you, you would usually look at the camera. Actors have to train themselves not to. Looking straight at the camera lens may spoil that take, and everyone on the set will have to start all over again.

Cell Phone Movie School

Place someone or something to focus on to one side of the camera. If you need to look to the other side during the same take, blink as your eyes pass the lens. That way you won't accidentally look at it.

Close, But Not Too Close

Your eyes are the most expressive part of your face. You need to make sure the camera can *see* the emotion in your eyes clearly, while still avoiding looking at the lens. The trick is to avoid looking at the area circled red (pictured left) and keep your gaze within the area circled green. If your eyes wander too far away from the camera, the audience will find it harder to connect to your thoughts.

Sometimes actors have to act opposite a cartoon or **CGI** creature that will be added to the movie later. When this happens, someone moves a stick with a tennis ball on the end to mimic the creature's movements. This gives the actors something to focus on!

Rules are made to be broken. Some directors intentionally "break the fourth wall" and ask actors to speak directly to the audience. The TV show *Malcolm in the Middle* used this technique.

WORKING IN FRONT OF THE CAMERA

Acting in front of a camera is a toned down version of acting on stage. Everything is done a little slower, a little quieter, and less exaggerated. Actors have to adjust how they act depending on what kind of camera shot the director wants, too. A **long shot** will need more exaggerated movements than a close-up, for example.

Acting For Different Camera Shots

Shot type	What's in the frame?	Acting required
Long shot	Camera sees you from head to toe at a distance	Make large gestures and expressions
Medium shot	Camera sees from your head down to the waist	Use small gestures and expressions
Close-up	Usually just all or part of your face, at close range	Acting must be subtle, don't exaggerate

Camera Acting Tips

- If you can't see the camera lens with both of your eyes, your head is probably turned too far away. Move your head in a little.
- When walking away or toward the camera, imagine there is an invisible, narrow path leading to the lens. This will keep you from wandering out of shot.
- Standing with your shoulders angled toward the camera looks more natural than standing straight-on.

When in a shot with another actor, look at them in the eye that is closest to the camera lens. Don't switch from eye to eye. It makes your character look shifty!

Cell Phone Movie School

Be aware of any habits you may have that might be distracting. Blinking, fidgeting, or playing with your hair can all become annoying quite quickly on film. Cut out any habits, unless you want them for your character.

WORKING ON SET

A movie set can be a bit of a scary place when you first start out as an actor. Everyone has a job to do and it is important to do your job as well as you can, and not cause any one else any problems.

Tips for Working on a Set

- If you stumble saying a line, keep going. It is up to the director to decide whether to stop or not.
- If you have questions about the shot, speak to the camera operator rather than the director. Directors can be very busy!
- Do not stop in the middle of a take for any reason.
- If you have ideas about your performance, speak to the director to make sure it is what they are looking for. Doing something unexpected may not be captured successfully.
- Make sure you know your lines and any movements you need to make. You will usually only get one rehearsal.

It can be nerve-wracking on set, but stay confident. The director chose you because they liked you for the part.

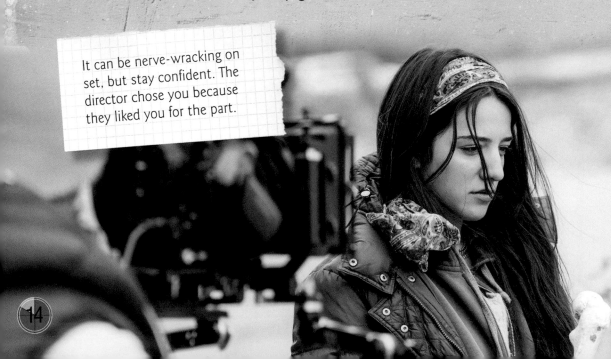

Hitting Your Marks

One of the most important parts of film acting is **hitting your marks**. Marks are usually pieces of colored tape in an "X" or "T" shape that have been carefully placed on the floor. The marks show you where to stand so you will be in focus in the shot. The camera operator needs you to be able to hit your mark perfectly.

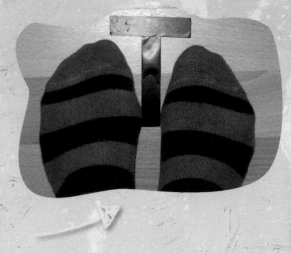

Cell Phone Movie School

It is not as easy as it sounds to hit your mark. You can't look down, as you are on camera. Try these tips. At rehearsal, look for something at eye-level that will tell you that you are at your mark. Perhaps an ornament comes into view at that point. If hitting your mark involves walking toward the camera while speaking, try walking backward from your mark before the cameras roll, saying your line. That way, when you walk forward again, saying your line, you will hit your mark exactly at the end of your sentence.

The camera department may have sausage-shaped markers that actors can use. These can be easier to find. The actor can feel them underfoot when they hit their mark.

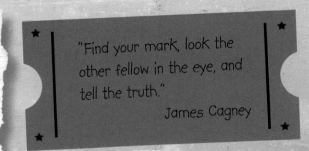

"Find your mark, look the other fellow in the eye, and tell the truth."

James Cagney

15

BEING CONSISTENT

Making sure things stay the same from take to take is called **continuity**. A scene is often shot from several different angles. Actors need to make sure that everything they do in each take will match up when the scene is edited together. For example, if they pick up a cup in their right hand in one take, they can't hold it in their left hand in the next take. The **script supervisor** is in charge of continuity. It is their job to help pick up any mistakes during filming.

Can you spot the continuity mistake in these two camera angles?

Can You Be Consistent?

Prepare a short scene to act. In the scene you must load a tray with several items, like in the photo above. Ask a friend to film you from three or four angles. Look back over the film from each camera angle. Did you get your continuity right? Did you always use the same hand to place each item? Did you put each item in the same spot? It is not as easy as it looks!

Actors also have to worry about continuity between different scenes. This is made even more difficult because movies are often shot out of order. If a movie has two scenes set in the same location, the director will almost always shoot them at the same time, even if they don't follow each other in the story.

This order switch can lead to continuity problems as it affects how an actor acts. If a character is shy at the beginning of the film but powerful by the end, the acting needs to show this.

Actors usually write notes on their scripts to remind them how their character is feeling in each scene.

Vincent is guilty, depressed, and angry. Patty's trailer was robbed, and he left it unlocked.

FADE IN:

EXT. TRAILER PARK - DAY

VINCENT and SARAH sit on their trailer steps.

VINCENT
Patty will be coming soo
We'd better clean up.

SARAH
She'll be mad.

VINCENT shrugs

SARAH (CONT'D)
Are you going to t

VINCENT
Gonna have to.

Cell Phone Movie School

Try filming three scenes from a play, once in order, and then once out of order. Rearrange the out-of-order recording using a video editing program such as iMovie, and then watch both versions back. Do the scenes flow as well in the one you filmed out of order?

LEARNING LINES

One of the most difficult things an actor has to do is learn their lines. By the time the cameras start to roll, actors have to be **off book**. Off book means knowing their lines word for word. We learn best when we are relaxed, so actors try not to get anxious about learning lines. If they find themselves feeling tense, they might take a bath, or go for a run. Then they tackle the script when they are feeling fresh again.

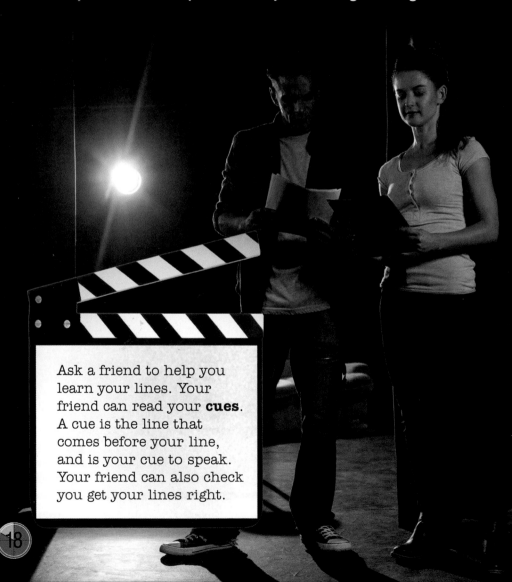

Ask a friend to help you learn your lines. Your friend can read your **cues**. A cue is the line that comes before your line, and is your cue to speak. Your friend can also check you get your lines right.

Helpful Tips to Make Learning Lines Easier

- Highlight your lines in the script.
- Break up the script into sections and learn them one at a time.
- As you learn each new section, go back over the earlier sections to keep them fresh in your mind.
- Write your lines. Writing uses another part of your brain and may help you learn lines faster.
- Say your lines aloud. Hearing your lines helps you memorize them faster.

- Practice how you are going to say your lines.
- Read your lines before you sleep. Our brain works while we sleep, so you get extra rehearsal time!
- Repeat difficult words over and over until you learn them.
- Before each day's filming, memorize your **sides**. Sides are just the pages of script you are shooting that day.

Cell Phone Movie School

Your smartphone can help you learn lines. You can video yourself saying your part. Then play back the video and say your lines along with the recording. Phone **apps** can also help you learn your lines. Off Book! lets you record your scene, and then **mute** your lines. As you play the scene back, you can rehearse by filling in the blanks.

"The whole essence of learning lines is to forget them so you can make them sound like you thought of them that instant."

Glenda Jackson

USING YOUR VOICE

As an actor, your voice is one of your most important pieces of equipment. Some actors earn a living just by using their voice. Voice actors might work on advertisements, cartoons, radio plays, and documentaries. Even when just doing a **voice-over**, actors might still move about. They will often act out a scene as if they are being filmed, as it helps them get into the part.

When acting in a movie or voice acting, the sound recordists microphones are never far away. It is important to speak at normal speaking volume. During an action scene, instead of shouting, actors might pronounce things with more **emphasis**, or speak faster, or talk in an intense whisper to get across a feeling of excitement or panic.

Actors that are used to performing on stage often find they talk too loudly when they first act in front of the camera.

Cell Phone Movie School

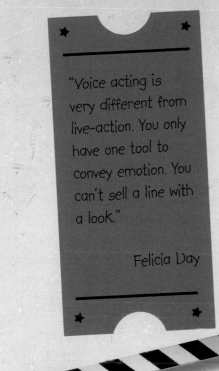

Actors need to look after their voices. Just as an athlete may warm up before a race, an actor should exercise their voice before performing. Try some of these voice **warm-ups**.

To help develop a strong voice, try this exercise. Start by doing a few big yawns. Slowly say "O" and "E" in a really exaggerated way. Feel your face really change shape as you say it. Say the letters over and over, and gradually speed up, until you run out of breath.

Never talk louder than the star of the movie. They set the volume for the scene, and they won't like it if you compete with them!

Try saying **tongue twisters** to help warm up your whole mouth. Tongue twisters are sentences that are especially difficult to say over and over, such as "unique New York" or "she sells seashells on the seashore." Try saying these without making a mistake. To warm up the **palate** and tongue, try saying, "Gooda, Gooda. Buddha, Buddha."

ACT NATURAL

So you've rehearsed your lines, and practiced hitting your mark. The cameras are ready. Now all you have to do is relax! Appearing relaxed in front of the camera is probably one of the hardest parts about acting. With so many things to remember, it's easy to look awkward and nervous.

Cell Phone Movie School

As an actor, it's important to know how to relax. Try breathing in through your nose while counting to four, hold for a count of seven, and breathe out through your mouth on a count of eight. Counting helps your brain concentrate on your breathing rather than whatever you are worried about.

Once you feel more relaxed, you could try taking another deep breath, raising your shoulders, and, as you breathe out, flop your body down like a rag doll. This helps relax your whole body, as well as your mind.

Using Business To Look Natural

Business is what characters do in a scene, such as typing on a keyboard, or making a sandwich. Doing things can really help make acting look more natural. Business doesn't have to be written in the script. You could just decide that instead of standing still, you will pick some fluff from your sweater while another character speaks.

The more real the business appears, the better it looks on camera. Really concentrate on getting all that fluff off your sweater! Business distracts you from concentrating too hard on your acting. Trying too hard can make your acting appear stiff and fake.

Adding business to a scene looks great, but it can cause continuity problems. Remember which hand held the pen, and at what point you picked it up and put it down again!

"Acting is all about honesty. If you can fake that, you've got it made."

George Burns

23

STUNTS AND COMBAT

In an action movie, actors may have to act out a fight scenes or do **stunts**. Stunts are dangerous or difficult feats, such as jumping off a building. **Stunt doubles** usually stand in for actors if the stunt or fight scene is dangerous. Stunt doubles are chosen to look like the actor they are playing. They are specially trained to perform action sequences safely.

Helmets, hats, or distinctive clothing can disguise the fact that it is a double doing the stunts.

Closely watch a movie action sequence. Can you tell when a stunt double takes the actor's place? There is usually a close-up of the real actor's face at the beginning and end of the scene, and the double does the action in between.

How to Throw a Stage Punch

Actors may do some stage fighting. One of the most common is to act as if they are either throwing or receiving a punch.

- First, actors measure their distance from each other to make sure the attacker's fist won't hit the victim.

- The camera is positioned behind the attacker's shoulder. The attacker throws a punch. On stage, the victim would clap their hands together as they react to the punch to make the sound effect. In a movie, a punch sound would usually be added later by the sound department.

- The camera angle makes it look as though the actors are much closer and the punch hits.

what the camera sees

Cell Phone Movie School

Try this pain-free tip to look as if one actor is really strangling another. The attacker put their hands around the victim's neck, and the victim grips the attacker's wrists. Now turn the scene on its head. Rather than strangling the victim, the attacker struggles to pull their hands away from the victim's grip, instead. Meanwhile, the victim tries to pull the attacker's hands toward them. This looks like a realistic struggle, but the victim is really in control all the time!

BECOMING AN ACTOR

Most actors start their careers by going to drama school. A few actors may begin acting on TV or in movies when they are children. Child actors usually belong to a drama group first, and then try out for roles in movies if they enjoy acting, and are good enough.

There are a lot of great out-of-work actors! If you really want to be an actor, don't let that get you down. You may have to do other work in between acting roles, though. Even the best Hollywood stars have spent months waiting tables until the next acting job comes along. It is sensible to have another job you can do, just in case.

These young actors are playing gangsters in a play.

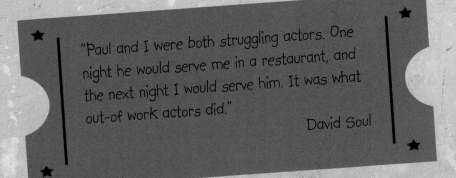

"Paul and I were both struggling actors. One night he would serve me in a restaurant, and the next night I would serve him. It was what out-of work actors did."

David Soul

Cell Phone Movie School

The best way to show filmmakers how good you are is to make a **showreel**. A showreel is a short collection of clips with examples of your best acting. You can make your own showreel using a smartphone. If you can, ask a friend to film you.

Include a mix of different acting, but keep the showreel short. Casting people are busy, and won't want to watch more than two to three minutes of clips. Don't be afraid to have some quiet moments in your showreel. Try to tell a story with your clips, to make it interesting and exciting for the people watching. Most importantly, only put your best acting in, leave out anything that you are not happy with. People will always judge a showreel by the worst part!

Whatever you do, make sure your showreel is shot in **landscape**, not **portrait** format.

 landscape   portrait

Real movies are filmed as landscape. A showreel shot in portrait looks amateur.

AUDITIONS

Casting **directors** usually choose the actors who play the parts in a movie. Sometimes casting directors will ask for actors to apply for a part by advertising in magazines, or on websites read by actors. They then look through actors' showreels and **resumés** to select people that might be suitable for the role. Then they will call the chosen actors for an **audition**.

Actors are always on the look out for their next role. It can be a full-time job searching for the next big part. Most actors have an **agent** who helps them find parts. Agents will know all the casting directors, and will get to hear about parts that may never be advertised.

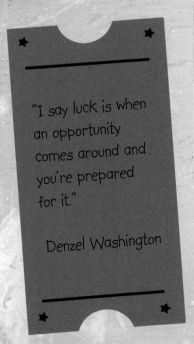

"I say luck is when an opportunity comes around and you're prepared for it."

Denzel Washington

Casting directors will be looking for very specific things, like a certain age and gender. Read advertisements for auditions very carefully to make sure you fit the part.

At the audition, actors may be asked to perform a scene they have rehearsed and memorized. Some auditions might ask actors to do a **cold reading**, where they perform a scene that they have never seen before.

Try not to chat to other people while waiting to audition. Spend the time relaxing and getting in character.

Cell Phone Movie School

Audition Tips:

• Be on time, ideally 15 minutes early.

• Make sure you are prepared and know your lines.

• Get to know the character you are playing.

• While you are waiting do some relaxation breathing, some tongue twister voice warm-ups, and practice reading your script out loud.

• Once in the audition, don't rush your lines. If you make a mistake, don't worry, just keep going.

• Only one person can get the role, and it may not be you. Never take a "no" to heart. Just get back out there and go for the next part.

GLOSSARY

agents A person who finds jobs for actors.

apps Applications.

auditions Short performances to test the talents of a musician, singer, dancer, or actor.

backstory A history or background created for a fictional character in a film or television program.

body language Movement or posture used as a means of expression.

business Any actions that an actor does while acting.

casting directors The people responsible for assigning roles in a film or play.

CGI Computer-generated imagery, or special visual effects created using computer software.

close-up Film image taken at close range and showing the subject on a large scale.

cold reading Reading aloud from a script or other text with little or no rehearsal.

continuity Consistency of details in the various scenes of a film.

cues A word, phrase, or action serving as a signal for the next actor to speak or do something.

emphasis Special attention or importance given to something.

fourth wall, the The imaginary "wall" that exists between actors and the audience.

hitting your marks Arriving correctly at marked points so as to be in camera shot, while acting.

landscape A format which is wider than it is high.

lighting technicians People responsible for setting up and controlling lighting on a movie set.

location Place away from a studio where a movie is shot.

long shot View of a scene shot from a considerable distance.

medium shot Camera shot in which the subject is in the middle distance.

movie set A place where some or all of a movie is produced.

mute To muffle or reduce the sound.

off book To know ones lines without needing to look at the script.

palate The roof of the mouth.

portrait A format which is taller than it is wide.

resumés Summaries of a person's working history.

script supervisor The member of a film crew who oversees the continuity.

showreel A short videotape of examples of an actor's or director's work for showing to potential employers.

sides The pages of the script that are being shot that day.

sound recordists The member of a film crew responsible for recording all sound.

stunt doubles Trained professionals who stand in for an actor in order to perform dangerous or physically demanding stunts.

stunts Exciting action in a movie that is or appears dangerous.

tone down Make less strong.

tongue twisters A sequence of words or sounds that are difficult to pronounce quickly and correctly.

voice-over A piece of narration in a film or broadcast, not accompanied by an image of the speaker.

warm-ups Preparation exercises before a performance.

FOR MORE INFORMATION

Books

London, Lisa. *From Start to Stardom - The Casting Director's Guide for Aspiring Actors.* Los Angeles, CA: Lisa London, Rochell Goodrich, 2014.

Stoller, Bryan Michael. *Smartphone Movie Maker.* Somerville, MA: Candlewick, 2017.

Websites

Due to the changing nature of Internet links, PowerKids Press has developed an online list of websites related to the subject of this book. This site is updated regularly. Please use this link to access the list:

www.powerkidslinks.com/mm/actors

INDEX

accents 9
action scenes 20, 24
agents 28
apps 19
auditions 28, 29

backstories 8
body language 9
Burns, George 23
business 23

Cagney, James 15
camera crew 4
camera operators 5, 15
casting directors 28
CGI 11
character 7, 8, 9, 17, 29
close-ups 7, 12
cold reading 29
continuity 16, 17, 23
costumes 5
cues 18

Day, Felicia 21
directors 4, 5, 6, 12, 14, 17

formats 27
fourth wall, the 10

habits 13
hair and makeup 5

iMovie 17

Jackson, Glenda 19

lighting technicians 4, 5
lines, learning 18, 19

locations 8, 17
long shots 12

Malcolm in the Middle 11
marks, hitting the 15
medium shots 12

off book 18, 19

rehearsals 14, 15
relaxing 18, 22, 29
resumés 28

sausages 15
scripts 17, 18, 19, 29
script supervisors 16
set, working on 14
showreels 27, 28
Shurtlef, Michael 8
sides 19
smartphones 5, 19, 27
Soul, David 26
sound recordists 4, 5, 20
stage acting 6, 7, 10, 20, 25
stage fighting 25
Streep, Meryl 5
stunt doubles 24
stunts 24

tongue twisters 21, 29

voice acting 20, 21
voice-overs 20

warm-ups 21
Washington, Denzel 28
Wittrock, Finn 7